EVERYDAY TALES OF
OLDER WOMEN
IN THEIR PRIME

Nicola Madge
Illustrations by Geo Parkin

Quadrant Books

Published in 2024 by Quadrant Books
A member of the Memoirs Group
Suite 2, Top Floor, 7 Dyer Street, Cirencester, Gloucestershire, GL7 2PF

Copyright ©Nicola Madge 2024

Nicola Madge has asserted her right under the Copyright Designs
and PatentsAct 1988 to be identified as the author of this work.

The moral right of the author has been asserted by them in
accordance with the Copyright, Designs and Patents Act, 1988

All rights reserved.

No part of this publication may be reproduced, stored in a retrieval
system, or transmitted in any form or by any means, without the prior
permission in writing of the publisher, nor be otherwise circulated in
any form of binding or cover other than that in which it is published
and without a similar condition including this condition being imposed
on the subsequent purchaser

Reasonable efforts have been made to find the copyright holders of
any third party copyright material. An appropriate acknowledgement can
be inserted by the publisher in any subsequent printing or edition

A catalogue record for this book is available from the British Library

Everyday Tales of Older Women in their Prime
Paperback ISBN 978-1-7398645-7-6

Illustrations by Geo Parkin

Printed and bound in Great Britain

About the author

Nicola Madge is a psychologist with a long career in social research and is currently Honorary Professor at Kingston University London. Recently she has turned her hand to poetry with this first volume. It is inspired by women's stories in Sixty Somethings. The lives of women who remember the Sixties (written with Paul Hoggart and published in 2020 by Quartet Books) as well as her own observations and imagination. To find out more about Nicola, visit her website at www.nicolamadge.co.uk

CONTENTS

Still going strong 1
Woman in her prime 2

Getting older 4
Image 5
Optimism 7
Oh dear 9

Keeping up appearances 11
Never too many 12
A new dress 14
Getting to the roots 16

A question of health 18
Just one glass 19
Keeping fit 21
Tuesday's tale 23
Excuses 24

The family 26
He's leaving home 27
Gran 29
Once upon a time 31
Staying put 33

Choosing a partner 36
I'll give it a go 37
Third time lucky 40
Marriage 42

Time for leisure	43
Keep travelling on	44
Wordle	46
The weekend	48

Sorting and tidying	51
Affairs	52
An impossible task	54
A spot of painting	57

The years tick by	59
Onwards and upwards	60
Everything	61
The endless cycle	63

Retirement	64
Finding the balance	65
The has-been star	67
The Puritan Ethic	69

Those were the days	72
My parents the beatniks	73
Homage to Ameliaranne and the Green Umbrella	75
Going modern	77

Resolution	80
A final fling – probably not	81

STILL GOING STRONG

Woman in her prime

Give me a fast car dye my hair
Watch me have another affair
I'm happy partying till late
See how I've become profligate

I'm up for anything you suggest
Outrageous and wild that's the best
Go on dare me and egg me on
So much to do before I'm gone

I plan to dance until I'm dead
Or climb Mount Everest instead
Bungee jump and trek abroad
Risk and adventure my reward

I like to shock that's really fun
Raising eyebrows second to none
I was meek and subdued before
But not at all now that's for sure

Indeed I'm braver and bolder
For every year I get older
What the heck I am forced to think
I'll do whatever makes me tick

While I still have the health and zest
My spirit will not be suppressed
Whenever my fires need a stoke
I'll pop pills and add rum to coke

A later life crisis perchance
No it's just sheer exuberance
Having fun if you are able
Keeps you going keeps you stable

So leave me be or do join in
I'm not stressed and there is no sin
Nothing is wrong it's just that I'm
A woman who is in her prime

GETTING OLDER

Image

Mirror mirror please tell me true
Just how old do I look to you
Mirror mirror what should I do
To make myself seem fresh and new

I'm fed up with this ageing face
Youth long lost with barely a trace
A less shapely waist hip and thigh
Oh why can't we our age defy

Of course some will say that we can
Selling false promises their plan
Dyes and creams and lotions many
Yours for just a pretty penny

Then there are procedures plenty
To turn you back to nearer twenty
Botox facelifts liposuction
Breast enlargement or reduction

All make claim to aid perfection
And of course ward off dejection
If one works try another too
If not have something else in lieu

Somewhat of a coward at heart
But thinking I might make a start
I book an appointment online
For the next morning half past nine

I see Donald a quack for sure
To seek advice on my allure
What can he do I meekly ask
Hoping it'd be a simple task

But of course I should have known
His comments would be overblown
No part of me did him impress
There was he said much to address

A tummy tuck or a nose job
And some other thingamebob
I might too try out brand new pills
Said to counter all types of ills

My self esteem was bad before
But now it had just hit the floor
I paid the bill and scuttled out
Full of angst and full of doubt

When I had got home however
And could reflect at my leisure
I realised things were not that bad
Nor was what I already had

My wrinkles show that I have smiled
Fought loved and even beguiled
And my worn in look does suggest
That I have lived life with a zest

So I'll remain just as I'm seen
A testimony to what's been
I am prouder of myself now
And even like my furrowed brow

Optimism

'How you can live longer' the headline read
She'd skip the dull news and peruse this instead
What would the latest bit of advice say
And would it be something that she could obey
Probably strategies for eating better and less
Sleeping more exercising and reducing stress

So it was with some surprise that she found
The requirement was actually more profound
It might lead to the same healthy conduct
But was based on a much broader construct
Optimism it heralded as the behavioural trait
That could often greater longevity create

The notion was attractive she was keen to try
To see if she could natural pessimism defy
She'd need to change the way she conceived
And see half empty cups as half full she believed
Recognizing too the silver linings behind clouds
And seeking out the smiling faces in crowds

She knew she would need to look the part
And continually smiling was a good start
Her vocabulary too she did transform
'Wonderful' and 'fantastic' becoming the norm
Her family remarked on her new found zeal
Secretly wondering what it might conceal

It went as well as could be hoped for a while
Even though she felt permanently on trial
And there was only so long she could pretend
That she could easily her behaviour amend
Black cats magpies and the number thirteen
Were constantly threatening to intervene

Much more comfortable with a measure of gloom
And a certain respect for the dangers that loom
She was used to these feelings in a strange sort of way
And they did her a *modus vivendi* convey
So at last she conceded with some dismay
She'd need another option her demise to delay

She couldn't handle optimism it was clear
Looking on the bright side wasn't for her
Worrying however did her avidly engage
And would hopefully conserve her to a ripe old age

Oh dear

Oh dear it seems I'm sixty eight
That does my mind so concentrate
How on earth can this really be
Is it almost curtains for me

Pull yourself together I say
There's still so much to come your way
Tasks aplenty fun and leisure
Don't let worry spoil your pleasure

Yes, that's it, I'll buy a new dress
Something that will my friends impress
I might even get a sexy top
And go on shopping till I drop

I'll also look in the recipe book
To find new platters I can cook
Keep up with all the latest trends
Serving vegan food to my friends

See films and plays, keep up to date
On the ball for any debate
Using rather than losing it
Exercising and keeping fit

So feeling good I venture out
To have fun I have no doubt
Amused by an advert displayed
'Get your mum off tinder' it said

Convincing myself I'm not old
And looking good so I am told
I trip around quite merrily
Fine at least temporarily

For it soon starts to unravel
As I press on with my travel
First I glance in a looking glass
Then I produce my old age pass

A thoughtful girl offers her seat
I take it but still feel a cheat
Later see the old people signs
Stooped and with their crooked spines

My feelings are quite mixed at best
Happy sad confused and the rest
It is all quite a conundrum
Am I old or am I still young

KEEPING UP APPEARANCES

Never too many

Nineteen twenty and still counting
Thirty one the toll is mounting
And that's just those that I can see
Piled on the shelves in front of me

They come in every shape and hue
Some old favourites some quite new
Made from leather wood or plastic
By and large they are fantastic

SHOES. We always have too few
And hanker after something new
Indeed those with pairs galore
Can always find the need for more

Sometimes indeed they must be bought
To take part in hobbies or sport
Dancing hiking even t'ai chi
Dictate just what footwear should be

Then we're concerned with appearance
Wanting style and coherence
Not prepared to feel downbeat
By having the wrong shoes on our feet

Do they match the outfit we wear
Have they the right amount of flair
Are the heels of the correct height
Do we in brief - well - look alright

It's thus not hard to speculate
How the pairs do accumulate
A friend once said one in one out
But that I do blatantly flout

How can I chuck what I've adored
Those red stilettos among the hoard
Or part with what may become vogue
Whether platforms boots or a brogue

On reflection I'll keep them all
I must admit I'm in their thrall
In fact I think I'll get some more
Lining shelves from ceiling to floor

Indeed I will go further still
Quite oblivious to the bill
And buy handbags to chaperone
Every pair of shoes that I own

A new dress

Getting frantic about what to wear
Choosing a dress fixing her hair
Years since the girls met had expired
Making an effort seemed required

They'd all be trying to look their best
And of course outdo the rest
The slimmest with best fashion sense
The chicest bag at any expense

And this was what she was dreading
Was it to shame she was heading
She didn't want to look a sight
Nor come over as just alright

Nonetheless she was out of touch
She didn't read magazines much
Maybe she'd seek her daughter's aid
Even though she'd likely upbraid

In the store the mother looked round
And soon she had four dresses found
The daughter looked on with disdain
She could not her approval feign

They're awful mum she blurted out
Unsuitable have no doubt
Too short too tight or too frilly
They'll all make you just look silly

The mother thanked for her support
And agreed they weren't what she sought
Nonetheless once her daughter fled
She did back to the shop then head

She bought the pink lacy number
That her body did encumber
She felt outrageous and pleased
All her anxieties had eased

There was no way she'd be a frump
And this dress at least would trump
T-shirts leggings and blue jeans
The bland uniform since their teens

If she couldn't win out on style
Perhaps she would make the girls smile
Call her mutton call her a tart
At least she'd be a figure of art

Getting to the roots

What shall I do about my hair
The roots are white the rest is fair
Should I accept my natural hue
Or do I tinting continue

As most ladies I have so far
Tried a perplexing repertoire
I've been blonde black redhead brunette
But nothing's seemed quite ideal yet

So maybe now the time is nigh
To at last abandon the dye
Hold my head up and so declare
I am grey now and I don't care

But then again I might regret
My foolhardiness and fret
It may be vainglory but yet
I don't want old age to abet

It's no good my mind is unclear
Isn't there any advice out there
No consensus is apparent
As confusion is inherent

Friends cite arguments con and pro
Colouring tresses as they grow
Can't stand chemicals and the fuss
Or staying youthful is a must

I can't decide I will postpone
Sorting this issue I do bemoan
I'd rather stay in a fine mess
Until I can this matter address

Meanwhile I can wear a chapeau
To hide the ugly roots that grow
Actually I don't care a fig
I'll just go out and buy a wig

A QUESTION OF HEALTH

Just one glass

Just one glass that's all it'll be
Quite enough for you and for me
We'll put the bottle out of sight
Not to touch it again tonight

And with that we served the meal
Happy as Punch we both did feel
An evening in what sheer bliss
We even shared a little kiss

The mackerel was quite divine
It went perfectly with the wine
The petits pois and sauce with thyme
Sweet potato fries all sublime

The table laid and napkins too
Ones with checks in red white and blue
Wood burner and candles alight
Soulful music that did delight

Everything as it should be
Romance and style for him and me
But alas we did want for more
Casting our eyes to the fridge door

I think it was me who first said
More wine or some water instead
It seemed that our resolve had gone
Was there an excuse to call on

We joked that the wine would go flat
And of course we couldn't have that
We thought it also might turn sweet
As the bottle was incomplete

And so it was we did agree
To have not two glasses but three
An extra bit won't do us harm
Quite the reverse we'll then stay calm

Anyway September's ending
And next month we are suspending
Drinking spirits wine and beer
To go sober for October

We'd tried before I do admit
But found it too much to commit
We're feeling stronger this time round
And will in future be allowed ... Just one glass

Keeping fit

I've joined the gym I do t'ai chi
I stretch and bend, the dog runs me
Stuck at home it's an indoor bike
Or hula hooping which I like

Yoga and pilates I do
Zumba and yes weight lifting too
Rolling on my big rubber ball
Press-ups sit-ups I try them all

I also swim and I do dance
Not knowingly missing a chance
To actively myself commit
And doing anything to keep fit

I sometimes wonder what it's for
And why I take on ever more
There's else to life do say my friends
But I retort it all depends

I'm getting older by the day
And want to remain just the way
I've always been in my mind's eye
Staying youthful, bendy and spry

Energy level, muscle tone
Making sure bingo wings have flown
I also want to remain well
And colds and infections repel

Lung capacity, heart rate
And of course keeping down my weight
So that's another reason why
With exercise I do comply

Cakes and biscuits I like best
But chocolate too – and the rest
My appetite does know no bounds
And thwarts attempts to shed the pounds

And so it is I do persist
All excuses promptly dismissed
I won't live for ever I know
But I'll give it a damn good go!

Tuesday's tale

I'm no sooner back from my holiday
Than it's to the dentist to take away
The tooth that is now far beyond repair
And only causing infection to flare

I sink back low in the black leather chair
And try to arrest any movement there
The surgeon's polite and puts me at ease
By talking about hobbies if you please

I then had to open wide and stay still
As she asked her assistant for the drill
Lying quite still I did not shake at all
Accepting just what to me would befall

The subsequent task was the extraction
Of the tooth that gave no satisfaction
After only five minutes it was out
Gosh that was easy I wanted to shout

Then I looked at what the dentist removed
And what I saw most absolutely proved
It was better out than in as she said
For its functional life was long since dead

Indeed there was no tooth and just three roots
Quite devoid of positive attributes
And simply debris that had lodged for years
Good riddance I thought as I shed no tears

Then with a gob in my mouth I drove home
No welcoming committee save the gnome
Happy apart from the single regret
Of zilch for the tooth fairy to collect

Excuses

It's a daily battle and not often that I win
Struggling with the pounds staying lithe and thin
The problem is I love my treats it's hard to turn them down
My excuses are legendary and have gained renown

All are well rehearsed and have stood the test of time
Some are quite ridiculous others just sublime
Overall however they couldn't be better picked
Being quite perfect as there's nothing they restrict

I eat when I'm upset so I can compensate
But also when I'm happy thereby to celebrate
There's always food on offer when in company
As well as lots to gorge on if I'm just with me

Staying at home in any case can be a sticky snare
Urging as it does raids on the Frigidaire
Also for succumbing to things naughty but nice
Best eaten up so they can no longer entice

Holidays are gratifying and a special case
With indulgences viewed as just commonplace
Weekends away can be quite wicked too
Dangling tasty temptations as they always do

Eating is a pleasure I'm very loth to reject
Cutting out bread and cakes would me quite deject
I don't mind holding back a teeny weeny bit
But anything more is a 'no no' I freely admit

Nicola Madge

So what I need to develop is a rationale
For a lifestyle that won't dent my morale
Maybe I could think up a really good excuse
For why I should my body continue to abuse

At my age I know I can't have gain without any pain
And that only my figure or face I can retain
Telling myself this makes it much more simple
To know just where I wish to make my committal

My best features are my visage and my smile
Feeling admired is what makes life worthwhile
If my cheeks start to droop and my eyes recede
I will surely become very miserable indeed

The logical decision then is to remain curvy
Sustained by eating whatever does please me
I won't make any pretence to being a saint
There's no point aspiring to what I certainly ain't

THE FAMILY

He's leaving home

Wiping the fresh tear from her face
She smiled and turned to embrace
Her son who was just leaving home
The last one to go it alone

She'd anticipated this day
When they'd all have gone away
With both sadness and elation
This day of their liberation

From then on her kids would decide
How their own lives would be applied
For her it meant freedom and time
To enjoy while still in her prime

All went well for a month or two
The kids were happy she was too
But then both she and their father
Began to miss fuss and laughter

They yearned for the daily spats
The tantrums and confiding chats
Everything was far too calm
Filling them with anxious alarm

So they went and bought a puppy
It was really a new baby
They could cuddle tend and adore
Clearing its messes from the floor

Being needed and loved again
Their contentment they could not feign
Time and freedom had them sated
Both were hugely over-rated

Gran

I'm the archetypal besotted Gran
And see my angel when I can
She's lovely gorgeous my sweet pet
Doubtless full of surprises yet

Happily I feed change and calm
Succumb completely to her charm
I melt under her softest touch
And do love her oh so so much

She gurgles, chuckles and gets cross
I think she knows who's truly boss
Her little fingers gripping me…
BUT did I say she's number three?

I adore the other two as well
Good and truly under their spell
Each with their special ways and wiles
All dished up with great heaps of smiles

I take to school I put to bed
I love it all it must be said
We cook and play and talk and doze
Listen to all their joys and woes

My daughters work their partners too
It seems they have a lot to do
I'm always free when there's a need
Answering the call with due speed

My name has morphed into Gran
I do feel valued by my clan
Everyone says I do my bit
But life has changed I must admit

The house a mess the larder bare
Horrible grey roots in my hair
Never have time for my best mate
And the garden's in such a state

Given up on that part-time job
Walk around looking quite a slob
Never make those museum trips
Everything in fact just slips

But I don't care a damn
I'm the archetypal besotted Gran

Nicola Madge

Once upon a time

Tell me about Cinderella once more
You know it's the story I most adore
My elfin granddaughter gave me a look
That sent me scuttling straightway for the book

I have found it Rose so hop on my knee
There's just time to read it before your tea
The tale is one of a poor young maid's plight
A servant despite her father onsite

The problem was her own mother had died
And the wealthy man had gained a new bride
She brought along her ugly daughters two
Who were mean and pathetic through and through

Now one morning and quite to their delight
Came an invite to a dance that same night
The sisters' boast that they would meet the Prince
Was just contrived to make poor Cinders wince

Somehow though Cinders did get to the ball
And there she did the Prince charm and enthral
They danced and embraced each other so tight
It was the most truly romantic sight

But alack and alas the clock struck midnight
And Cinders set off in immediate flight
She sped away but in haste lost a shoe
Which to her identity was the only clue

The love-struck beau was utterly distressed
To suddenly lose the girl he'd caressed
He sought high and low the love of his life
His only concern to make her his wife

The glass shoe was to be tried on by all
To find the foot not too big nor too small
The ugly sisters were loth to admit
That it very clearly did not them fit

Cinders was hiding but came into view
And insisted she should try it on too
Lo and behold it was just the right size
The Prince proposed and the rest we'll surmise

I love that story smiled my little Rose
But is it plausible nobody knows
Mulling my reply she did intervene
With a request for jelly and ice cream …

Staying put

Mum you should now give up the house
It's far too big without your spouse
Bro and I have left home as well
Definitely the time to sell

The daughter continued to try
To get mum to see eye to eye
With what she thought would suit her too
Maybe help her income accrue

The mother later pondered hard
She knew she must stay on her guard
There were no rooms she didn't use
And she would do what she did choose

Her choice was against removal
But with family approval
Best to go through the motions though
And great enthusiasm show

The estate agent was called in
To give her all the normal spin
A fine house he quickly said
Sell with us we're streets ahead

She took him on put up a sign
But to viewers she drew the line
Looking too at places to buy
Whether distant or nearer by

Then she called her children round
To update them on what she'd found
She told them of the likely sale
But what she next said turned them pale

She thanked them first for their concern
And said she'd not their advice spurn
Luckily she had found a lair
A bijou mews house in Mayfair

Their faces crumbled as they gasped
They kept their fists tightly clasped
How would they now get out of this
And could they this new plan dismiss

It's quite lovely she did avow
And much better than what I've now
How clever you both were to see
What will really be right for me

But mum they said to interrupt
Moving will your life so disrupt
Maybe we were hasty after all
Perhaps we did make the wrong call

No no my dears, the mother smiled
Mayfair has me truly beguiled
It won't cost much more than I'll get
I doubt I will go into debt

In any case I have stocks and shares
Which I can sell to do repairs
My savings too can be of use
And my pension I can reduce

Horrified the sibs swapped glances
What honestly were their chances
Of slowing their mother's tempo
And persuading her not to go

Mayfair's too far away they cried
We'll paint the house they also lied
We erred and think you should stay put
Please say your plan is now kaput

The mother winked out of their sight
She heaved a sigh and said alright
You are my children you know best
Yes I will keep our family nest

CHOOSING A PARTNER

I'll give it a go

I used to think I needed men
But this is now and that was then
Being free doing my own thing
I'm very happy without a ring

I've been married not once but twice
It wasn't always worth the price
There was fun but also much pain
Don't think I'll ever do it again

For being alone is a plus
More serene and far less fuss
Make decisions take my own stand
Nobody there to reprimand

Go to bed at half past seven
Up in the morn after eleven
Eat baked beans out of the tin
Have my nightcap of pure gin

All the same I do sometimes miss
A long cuddle and goodnight kiss
Perhaps I just hadn't found Mr Right
My paramour my shining knight

Maybe I should have one more try
To find true love before I die
My friend tells me it'd do me good
Indeed she says I really should

Okay then I'll give it a go
Look online to search for a beau
I'm not after great looks or style
Or even someone whose made a pile

A kind and thoughtful friend I'd choose
Not a bloke given to the blues
Also of course a great lover
Faithful to me forsaking all other

So now I must make a clear plan
For how I'm going to hook my man
There's so much choice too many sites
Where can I hope to find delights

There are those for singles divorcees
Interest groups or retirees
Sites for love or fun on the side
Same sex mixed sex other implied

I go for 'second time arounds'
Hope it's better than it sounds
Well why not it's as good as any
Especially when there are so many

I write my profile choose a name
Submit and play the waiting game
I won't be making a first move
Instead responding to approve

To my complete utter surprise
I get messages from two guys
Both seem alright from what they say
I think replying is okay

One very quickly shrinks from sight
Maybe something that I did write
The other seems quite keen to meet
And says a meal would be his treat

I do concur a date is set
I'm not sure what I'm feeling yet
But on the day the signs are good
And I do feel properly wooed

One month later still going strong
Getting better as time goes on
Nonetheless it remains the case
That we just have to watch this space

It's hard to say where it will go
But I've now realised one thing though
In terms of men without a doubt
I'm better with one than without

Third time lucky

Goodness gracious Martha's to wed
Third time lucky I'm told she said
Great she's got a sense of humour
If there is truth in this rumour

Her first husband was a charmer
But the marriage a non-starter
He'd lots of ladies on the side
But when confronted always lied

It all came to a head one day
When Martha said she'd gone away
Unemployed and randy to boot
He did a young lady recruit

So when she returned to surprise
She baulked at what then met her eyes
The two of them in her bed lay
No excuses could they convey

After him she married again
Seemingly opting for more pain
At first the groom pampered and fussed
Gaining her unquestioning trust

He next set up a joint account
From which he spent a vast amount
Once her assets had disappeared
He left with what he'd commandeered

Nicola Madge

After these two tales of woe
Why would she want another beau
I've now from her the reason wrest
And possibly I should have guessed

In older age she's right off men
It's same sex marriage with Bronwen
So let's hope it's an end to strife
And she's not more than thrice a wife

Marriage

What is the secret of a happy marriage
We're often asked as if we could really say
Just 'cos we've been together for many years
Doesn't mean we have much of use to relay

We've had ups and downs as all couples do
But have always managed to string along
In arguments we are prepared to let go
And to freely admit it when we're wrong

Turns are taken at the ironing board and sink
We can both make lunch or boil an egg
Money is managed with never a stink
And neither minds the other pulling a leg

We're also quite matched in leisure time
With intimate moments and shared attention
But is everything so perfect you may opine
Is there not a catch I may need to mention

The catch of course is the operative word
As once I caught him and he also caught me
We chose the best as you have probably heard
And of course the rest is mere h-i-s-t-o-r-y

TIME FOR
LEISURE

Keep travelling on

Ladies who age often acquire
A new and rather odd desire
Not a red dress nor fancy man
No indeed it's a camper van

Remembering their youthful days
A hippy and carefree phase
When reason was an afterthought
And excitement was what was sought

To travel then was paramount
Constrained of course by bank account
Only the lucky ones could afford
To be in a camper van abroad

Iconic was the VW
White maroon or turquoise blue
Split screen pop top rock and roll bed
Or bay window and tin top instead

It all seems so romantic now
Gone are memories of just how
Uncomfortable it had been
With rooftop beds and loos unclean

Also progress was precarious
Even if quite hilarious
Out of petrol suspension bent
Miles from anywhere francs all spent

Nicola Madge

A trip was quite an enterprise
That had its lows and had its highs
With no recourse to mobile phone
Problems had to be fixed alone

Nowadays the standards are higher
Ladies their comforts do require
Proper washrooms and decent meals
A cosy bed despite the wheels

Key as well a relaxing drive
Parking sensors and satnav live
Extra gears bluetooth air con
And roadside help to call upon

Adventure's still possible though
For ladies with get up and go
So if you're truly game and set
It's hard to match the thrill you'll get

Wordle

I have a new incentive for getting up each day
Which is to do the word game that millions play
Solving Wordle early on is my excuse for delay
In getting more necessary tasks underway

The aim of the game is to attempt to surmise
A word with five letters in up to six tries
The word initially up front is a total guess
But thereafter it's a mix of luck and finesse

Choosing a word from my cluttered mind
Is as good as any other wake-up call I find
I type my letters and then press display
Not overconfident I'll have the right array

I'm fascinated by the draw of the game
Enticing numerous pundits into the frame
That's why the New York Times has blown
Loads of dosh to make Wordle its own

Five of my family are on WhatsApp where
We proudly (or not) our daily scores compare
We say we're not in it for the competition
But well I suppose we are just a smidgeon

There was only one time we did complain
And luckily it hasn't so far happened again*
The American spelling of favor was once used
Leaving us truculent and somewhat confused

It is a simple game to be enjoyed by all
And that's why we are so much in its thrall
Great tease enjoy angst blast or bravo
What'll be my winning word to-mor-row?

*It has now

The weekend

Her Let's do something different today
Be adventurous break away
Not just follow our weekend norm
Please for once let us not conform

That's not to say I don't adore
Everything we have done before
It's just that we should have a change
Do new things to extend our range

Him Yes I do perfectly agree
I can your point completely see
Something different would be great
It'd refresh us and elate

So what do you think we should do
If we're our routine to eschew
Options aplenty to amuse
The challenge is having to choose

Her My mind is a blank let me think
What might really tickle us pink
I'll check Time Out and search online
For fun to which we do incline

Him I've an idea what do you say
About a trip to the ballet
There's a performance on right now
Well reviewed but not too highbrow

Her Well yes I suppose we could go
Although again well I don't know
The weather's fine a lovely day
Not sure we want to hide away

Him Do you then fancy a fun run
We'd be al fresco in the sun
It's still not too late to embark
On the jogging race in the park

Her A good idea but I'm not sure
I could all that running endure
We're out of training and what's more
I guess we would the heat deplore

Him Then what about the outside pool
It's in fresh air and we'd stay cool
Surely that's the best idea yet
Fun relaxing not too much sweat

Her I know I'm being too picky
But it would be somewhat tricky
For my bikini is too tight
I don't want to excite or fright

Him Okay well we could go to shops
To buy you some bottoms and tops
We've not yet been to that new mall
Where I'm sure they have got it all

Her But today's not good to be there
There'll be crowds no room to spare
And furthermore car parks are full
I don't think we'd like it at all

Him	Well you come up with something then
	I have tried again and again
	To please but every suggestion
	Has been ruled out of the question
Her	I'm sorry I am so annoying
	And admit I am now toying
	With calling our search to an end
	And just enjoying our weekend
	Let's do what we usually do
	Not plan anything else in lieu
	Clean up shop cook and whatever
	Just so long as we're together

SORTING AND TIDYING

Affairs

My friend says she's sorting out her affairs
What? With George or Fredrick or Mike? I crow
She turns towards me and quite simply glares
That's not what I mean as well you do know

Well I take the hint and I'll do mine too
She has a point and it can't be that hard
I don't want to leave the kids in a stew
Should the grim reaper catch me off guard

But my resolution is not good enough
This is not how I should be spending my time
Why should I think about this boring stuff
While I am still a woman who is in her prime

Unfortunately common sense does prevail
I shall update my will as the task for today
But it's harder than I thought and I sadly fail
Indecision on allocation forces delay

Maybe instead I'll set up Powers of Attorney
My son says I need them and I'd better comply
One for my welfare and one for my money
For if I become doolally before I die

Gosh this is so depressing where's the fun
Is this all life's about at my ripe old age
Must I get filing and spreadsheets done
Are my last years sadly doomed to be beige

No I can be only who I have been
Somewhat a rebel but caring as well
I shall try to be helpful to my kin
But also focus on tasks that compel

Maybe I should endeavour to discard
The bundles of *billets doux* in the chest
I'll untie the red ribbons and re-regard
The letters that once had my heart caressed

They are surely not for my children's eyes
But once more I will read them through
Then into the shredder for their demise
- Although I might just keep one or two

My friend calls to see what I'm about
She proudly jokes she is ready to die
As she has created order throughout
And is now feeling gleeful and high

I ponder what my retort would best be
Opting for a little less than the truth
I've done all I can I state honestly
And dealt with affairs right back to my youth

An impossible task

I just don't know where I should start
It's really easy to lose heart
The cupboards full no space at all
Stuff everywhere wall to wall

There's an issue in every room
Even where one might well assume
Things in order nothing amiss
Without opening the drawers that is

And even in the hallway too
Gloves of every possible hue
Bulging coat racks wellington boots
Things galore for outdoor pursuits

The truth is that it's out of hand
As o'er the years we did expand
Far too much stuff we now possess
Yes a veritable excess

Now and then I make some attempt
To transform from chaos to kempt
But all the while that I have tried
The stuff has only multiplied

It seems I can't do it alone
The task has now so overblown
Marie Kondo I do mutter
Please please help me to declutter

But no that's not realistic
I must be more optimistic
I'll set a task for every day
And sort the problem in that way

I'll go and buy some coloured sacks
To put clothing books and knick knacks
For the dump or charity shop
Those to chuck give away or swap

My good intentions spur me on
And to the shop I go anon
Buy bags of yellow green and blue
Determined to see the job through

Full of confidence for success
I set to clearing up the mess
It's not long though before I find
That I have become disinclined

I came unstuck from the word go
Not finding much that I could throw
Everyone has a claim to make
And things are kept for old time's sake

The trouble is that souvenirs
Remind of joys across the years
That brooch from Gran a child's first shoe
A wedding gift a pot I threw

Other objects have some worth
Indeed there seems really no dearth
Of things we're keeping just in case
There's something they can well replace

Then things that are handy and small
Surely we could keep them all
A bag of nails and two rawl plugs
A tin whistle a few old mugs

But lightbulbs we have no fittings for
They should go that's for sure
Well what a waste you never know
They might set someone's lamp aglow

After three days of trying hard
My plan I had to disregard
It was clear that I had failed
Just as another thought prevailed

I wanted my house in good order
Despite the fact I'm a hoarder
So in the end my goal instead
Became to build a garden shed

A spot of painting

A ray of sunshine creeps across the room
Highlighting and caressing the winter gloom
But now it's spring I must tidy and renew
Transform my home to a more welcome hue

So breakfast's done and it's off to the town
To buy some paint either Dulux or Crown
Plus assorted brushes and a scraper
Masking tape turps and rough sandpaper

I start on the hallway that's frankly dire
And work so hard that I soon perspire
First I take the bikes out to the shed
Where from now on they'll live instead

I must also remove the nail from the wall
The broken cable will have to go and all
They'll spoil the look if they stay in place
They need to be gone without a trace

I labour all day and well into the night
It's all starting to look airy and bright
Well that's before the ear-splitting scream
That signals the end of my DIY dream

The cats are cross and have got into a fight
Hissing and clawing with all their might
Then there is a chase to the front door
Which knocks the paint pot onto the floor

What a mess!

Not only the floor but the painted walls too
Are covered in the horrible sticky goo
This is not the effect I had been looking for
So no tangible benefit from my arduous chore

Expletive deleted!!

THE YEARS TICK BY

Onwards and upwards

Now it isn't exactly as I had been told
This dastardly process of growing old
I feel much the same as when twenty four
If anything I'm now enjoying life more

My carriage is still more or less upright
And I have hearing sense of smell and sight
It's true crow lines crawl across my face
But I wouldn't for the world them erase

They're testimony to pain and pleasure
Reflecting family work and leisure
A full life is no blessing in disguise
It is indeed the most sought after prize

But it's still far from over I earnestly hope
And I'll seize the day while I can yet cope
My bucket list is an enormous pail of desire
Of everything to do before I expire

Ablaze with energy I just don't seem to tire
And I'm generally unused to worry and fear
But I am rattled when the grim reaper comes near
Jumpy and twitchy until the coast is again clear

On the whole though my current life is great
I am after all only seventy eight

Everything

Shakespeare wrote of seven ages
As our lives do turn the pages
From helpless babe to school age child
Then teenager by sex beguiled

Young adulthood is the next role
Entered into with heart and soul
Passionate and ambitious
Adventurous and capricious

Middle age is not far behind
A time to feel wise and refined
Confident and with a girth that grows
And an age that respect bestows

Becoming old is next in line
When influence is in decline
Losing weight and voice and all
Nobody much still is in thrall

Then the final stage edges nigh
Tasked to dotage and death defy
The bard suggests it's more or less
Oblivion and childishness

Indeed he's very explicit
Really not much to exhibit
Sans teeth sans eyes sans taste he deems
Indeed ***sans*** everything it seems

But an objection must be raised
And this life stage now reappraised
It may not be the same these days
We have our wills we have our ways

So those who have the means to pay
Can strive to keep old age at bay
There're plenty after our money
Selling us their milk and honey

And we can be self improvers
Through restrictions and manoeuvres
Eat with care and cut the booze
Go for walks and chase the blues

It is of course merely delay
The reaper will still have his way
But until then we sure will cling
To being *avec* everything

The endless cycle

It becomes easy to forget the cold days past
With longer glimpses of sunshine at last
More comfortable as it starts to get warm
The landscape energised to transform

The birds on the fence tweet their delight
As snowdrops and crocuses come into sight
Trees that were bare display new shoots
The bees wake up the ants gain recruits

The direction is from winter to spring
And in its wake does new sounds bring
The horses whinny and the donkeys bray
While the gambolling lambs bleet all day

Even the farmer's sigh is more muted
As the endless darkness become diluted
By visible stains of light high in the sky
And frost and ice have since passed by

He no longer jokes about a medal earned
And doesn't despise what's been adjourned
The system that propels the seasons on
Will introduce summer before too long

Feeling gladdened he will tool the land
Enjoying nature's splendours at first hand
But alas spring will be gone as it came
And all too soon it will be winter again

Which means another precious year has gone ...

RETIREMENT

Finding the balance

I've worked blooming hard all my life
Carrying on as mum and wife
It seemed that I could have it all
No job too big, no task too small

Up at dawn, sandwiches to make
Never forgot that birthday cake
Washing done while cooking the meal
Helping with homework, no big deal

Rushing to work, and never late
Up before six, home after eight
Writing reports, appeasing the boss
Keeping accounts, not getting cross

I strove for work life balance too
And never did my kids eschew
Talking, playing, fetching from friends
Trying hard and making amends

Hubby too was not forgotten
I did love him something rotten
Guests for dinner, outings as treats
Keeping fit for under the sheets

When I think back I am aghast
How long did I think it could last
Keeping up with the latest trends
Burning the candle at both ends

But all the same I did still fret
Checked out 'retirement' on the net
What would I do when my job stopped
And the kids from home had hopped

Would I be bored, sad and bereft
Feeling little in life was left
Would I be past my sell-by date
Having lunch and putting on weight

NO, I couldn't have been more wrong
I'm glad I didn't work prolong
Life balance didn't exist then
Not for the women in my ken

The message had been quite deceiving
We chored all day and all evening
Far better now that I can choose
What to do and what to refuse

The has-been star

The stream of water on her hair
Was just as hot as she could bear
Her silver locks felt soft and warm
She'd soon be ready to perform

It was many years since her last act
Twenty seven as a matter of fact
But now she had a part in a play
And the rehearsal would be today

Applying some oil then to her face
With a cloth she managed to erase
Some wrinkles and the cross brow line
That did her vivacious life define

After an adjustment to her dress
And most excited she did confess
She went to the theatre to re-invent
The career for which she was meant

But all was not as she had dreamed
There'd been an error sadly it seemed
So sorry love did the director exclaim
There was a confusion with your name

The role had not been for her after all
But alas to another it did befall
It was a blow there was no doubt
A familiar reminder of what acting's about

But the crew and cast were very kind
And she was lavishly wined and dined
A harmonious end to a disappointing day
Although secretly she was glad in a way

After all she had had fortune and fame
And much acclaim when top of her game
She wouldn't her fine reputation mar
By appearing as some ageing has-been star

The Puritan Ethic

The Puritan Ethic lives on
Long after days of work are gone
Imperative, instilled and set
Something we can never forget

So even when we do retire
We still have that strong desire
To give meaning to our lives
And cope with whatever arrives

We seem to need a routine still
Advance notice of things to fill
The coming day, next week, next year
Tasks to keep our conscience clear

Do not however get me wrong
There is some scope to play along
With defining both work and play
To ensure things, well, go our way

A late morning lie-in, let's say
Is just because we need to stay
In good health in body and mind
Which means enough time to unwind

And meeting friends for a natter
That does for our welfare matter
The pizza really just a perk
Of maintaining our old network

Doing the rounds of shops and stores
Gets us moving and outdoors
Looking at whatever's for sale
Ensures we never do get stale

And reading novels before tea
Is not the sin it's said to be
Crosswords, quizzes and puzzles too
Sharpen our minds and old age eschew

Even having a nip and tuck
Doesn't mean we have come unstuck
We're told the value of self esteem
And we're just realizing our dream

I could go on making the case
Why it's important to embrace
A broad-minded view of what
Really matters and what does not

It revives that question of yore
What were our lives given us for
What does being productive mean
And when do we ourselves demean

Needs and duties change as we age
With new concerns at every stage
In later life we should not forget
There's time to enjoy ourselves yet

So let's be 'useful' when we can
Helping others within the plan
But in the time that remains spare
Do what we like it's only fair

Nicola Madge

No need to feel guilt or remorse
As others would likely endorse
Do those things that we've never done
Embrace them now and have some fun

Paint the town red or remain blue
It's up to us what we do
Forget the ironing and play
Tasks can wait for another day

THOSE
WERE THE
DAYS

My parents the beatniks

If I have rather strange ideas
Differing somewhat from my peers
It may be down to mum and dad
And the upbringing that I had

I say mum and dad as one word
As which was which was sometimes blurred
Indeed they were about the same size
And both wore dark glasses over their eyes

A black turtle neck and a French beret
Completed the look and did betray
Their identity have you guessed
Well my parents were beatniks yes

I had a very happy childhood
And I'd have it again if I could
Always on somebody's shoulder or hip
Always taken along on any trip

So no, I was not at all neglected
But my learning was certainly affected
I went out on protests not to the park
And could identify marijuana in the dark

My first words too gained me aplomb
Square and cool and Ban the Bomb
We ate Vesta Curry as we marched
And drank coca cola when we were parched

I wasn't read Noddy and Big Ears at bedtime
But was fed a diet of poetry and rhyme
I soon learned to dig Brubeck and Getz
And still listen to them now so no regrets

Which brings us back to where I began
To the reasons why I am what I am
My bongo drums and loafers are with me still
And clams from a tin always give me a thrill

Homage to Ameliaranne and the Green Umbrella

I had a book when I was small
That did me utterly enthral
T'was about a girl called Ameliaranne
And this oh reader is how it began

She was the oldest of a large brood
In a family often short of food
Loving her siblings a great deal
She resolved to find them a meal

Her chance came with a surprise invite
To a fine party that very night
It was a pity her sibs were not asked too
But she decided what she would do

Plucking the green umbrella from its stand
Her true reward was close at hand
The mother said it wasn't likely to rain
But doubts about that she was forced to feign

Looking in the mirror to check her curl
She did then depart and her adieus hurl
For Ameliaranne was now set to ensure
She would goodies for her family procure

Her visit proved a great success
For reasons you can probably guess
Everything she was given to eat
She popped in the brolly for a later treat

When it became full and an awful weight
She left so as not to be too late
To get back to her family in time for tea
Which would be as good as could be

As she opened the umbrella in front of all
Sandwiches cakes and sweets did fall
Her brothers and sisters had no need to plead
As there was plenty for them all to feed

I loved that book and would read it again
Which is where the de-cluttering comes in
It's somewhere lost in a box in the loft
And that's a spidery place I don't go oft

Going modern

What would I do without my mobile phone
It keeps me amused when I'm home alone
It has become my companion and friend
To whom else would that compliment extend

I can talk to my children round the world
To see if they're doing as they've been told
Also check where they are and wish them well
Make sure they're alright as if they would tell

I can watch the news that's hot off the press
Be warned of issues to quickly address
Buy some loo rolls before the shelves run bare
Know this season's correct colour to wear

Music is just at the touch of the screen
Access something new or my faves as a teen
Anything else I ask Google about
And by magic the answer is churned out

All this is available and much more
Alarm clock calculator apps galore
We can do our shopping and pay our bills
The camera takes videos and stills

So what a crisis when our phone is lost
A new one a must whatever the cost
How did we manage without this device
Were we not aware of our sacrifice

But when I ponder this question further
And upon my life become observer
It is clear that with gains come losses too
There are so many things we can't now do

In our younger days learning wasn't quick
No internet enquiry with just one click
We would have to investigate and read
Expend time and due diligence indeed

Maybe there was something to be said
For having to make such effort instead
We had to know tables and parts of speech
Have logarithms and a slide rule each

Now too there are few surprises to glean
Wherever we go it's already been seen
Much more exciting when we were young
To have some novelty upon us sprung

Also worse now is that lives are on view
With all the implications that ensue
We're always on call and pay the price
There's no excuse with a mobile device

I think I shall stop reminiscing now
As although nostalgic I do avow
That I sure want to keep my mobile phone
It's a lifeline to not feeling alone

Nicola Madge

I'm very content with my current life
With all its pleasures and all its strife
Furthermore I know when to keep quiet
And not provoke friends and family to riot

I won't say things once were better for fear
That I'll just be labelled a poor old dear

RESOLUTION

Nicola Madge

A final fling – probably not

A new year means a new you we are told
And this time yes I'm going to be bold
With no intention of growing old with grace
My resolution is to excitement embrace

I've decided to be outrageous and wild
After all I must prove I'm a Sixties child
Ordinary is out and really so last year
And now it's to hedonism I will adhere

So my heart please lead me astray
And find me a toy boy with whom to play
Let him be beautiful funny and louche
So our affair can go with a whoosh

I also plan to swap navy blue clothes
For lacy pink dresses with orange hose
Hoping to cause a stir and catch the eye
I'll be wearing stilettos six inches high

And then I will party all day and night
Not giving in to fatigue without a fight
My favourite tipple will be champagne
From which I'll find it hard to abstain

It may not be easy but I won't let on
And I'll keep going until the year is gone
Only then will I relax and quietly smile
Leaving behind twelve months of guile

You are yourself again my friends will say
We were worried your life was in disarray
I know I'll have become a shadow again
But after a year of high jinx I won't complain

www.ingramcontent.com/pod-product-compliance
Lightning Source LLC
Chambersburg PA
CBHW011315080526
44587CB00024B/4012